Tallinn
TRAVEL
GUIDE
2023

An itinerary guide to Tallinn's exploration,
cuisine, top hidden gems in 2023.

Dan C. Bernardi

Table of Contents

INTRODUCTION

The lovely capital of Estonia, Tallinn, is a place where modernism and heritage coexist harmoniously. This charming European location, located on the Baltic Sea's northern coast, has a bustling atmosphere, medieval architecture, and a rich cultural legacy. We'll go into great detail about Tallinn in our travel guide, giving you all the details you need to organize an enjoyable trip to this charming city.

1.1 About Tallinn

Everyone who visits Tallinn is enthralled by the city. Danish crusaders founded it in the thirteenth century, which is when it first appeared. Tallinn has been shaped by a number of cultures over the years, including the Hanseatic League, Sweden, and Russia, all of which have an impact on the city's architecture, customs, and culture. Tallinn's Old Town, a UNESCO World Heritage site and a symbol of the city's historical importance, is its most recognizable feature.

The Old Town, or "Vanalinn" in Estonian, is a labyrinth of medieval structures, Gothic spires, and cobblestone streets. You'll feel as though you've traveled back in time as you stroll through this beautifully preserved medieval district. You may tour ancient locations like Town Hall Square, Toompea Castle, and Alexander Nevsky Cathedral. The city's distinctive attractiveness results from the blending of its historical riches with a cutting-edge, progressive civilization.

Tallinn has a wide variety of attractions available outside of the Old Town. Peter the Great established Kadriorg Palace and Park, which is a spectacular example of baroque architecture set within lovely gardens. The Kumu Art Museum and the Estonian Maritime Museum are just a couple of the many galleries and museums the city has to offer. The many parks and green areas, like Pirita Beach and the Lahemaa

National Park nearby, are a haven for nature lovers.

1.2 Planning Your Trip

To ensure a successful and pleasurable trip to Tallinn, careful planning is essential before you leave. Here are some crucial factors to remember:

1.2.1 The Best Time to Visit: Tallinn has a variety of seasons, with warm summers and chilly winters. The greatest time to go is in the summer, from June to August, when the weather is nice and the city is bustling with festivals and outdoor events. If you prefer a winter paradise, don't pass up the chance to visit Tallinn's enchanted Christmas markets in December.

1.2.2 Length of Stay: Depending on your interests, a trip to Tallinn should last as long as possible. A weekend is enough time to take in the Old Town and some of the major sights. Consider staying 3 to 5 days to get a more in-depth experience, and leave time for day visits to surrounding places.

1.2.3 Lodging: Tallinn has a variety of lodging choices, from opulent hotels to affordable hostels and inviting guesthouses. It's a good idea to make reservations in advance, especially during the busiest travel period.

1.2.4 Travel: Tallinn is easily accessible by air, sea, and land. The primary entry point for tourists from other countries is Tallinn Airport. Trams, buses, and trolleys are all part of the effective public transportation infrastructure in the city, which makes getting about simple. If you want to travel outside of the city, you can rent a car, and the train and ferry systems provide you access to other regions of Estonia and neighboring nations.

1.3 Essential Travel Tips

Here are some crucial travel suggestions to have in mind in order to make sure you have a wonderful and trouble-free vacation to Tallinn:

1.3.1 The Euro (EUR) is the official currency of Estonia. There are several ATMs across the city, and credit and debit cards are commonly accepted.

1.3.2 The official language of Estonia is Estonian, but English and Russian are increasingly widely used, especially in tourist areas. Locals can benefit from learning a few fundamental Estonian phrases.

1.3.3 Security: Travelers can feel safe in Tallinn most of the time. Nevertheless, it is advisable to exercise caution and follow the standard safety procedures, such as protecting your property and avoiding dimly lit or isolated areas at night.

1.3.4 Local food: Take advantage of the chance to sample Estonian food. Consider traditional fare like kama, black bread, and herring. The city is renowned for its thriving craft beer scene and café culture.

1.3.5 Electrical Outlets: Type F outlets, which are the European Union standard, are used in Estonia. Bring the proper adapters if your devices use a different type of plug.

In sum, Tallinn is a city of fascinating contrasts where ancient history and modern culture coexist together. Remember to immerse yourself in the distinctive experiences that this Baltic treasure has to offer when you make travel plans. Tallinn delivers a voyage full of unique experiences and priceless memories, from seeing the Old Town's historic alleyways to indulging in regional cuisine. Enjoy your exploration of the fascinating capital of Estonia.

GETTING TO TALLINN

Once you've made the decision to travel to Tallinn, knowing how to get there is crucial for a straightforward and pleasurable trip. The numerous modes of transportation, information about the city's airports and terminals, and the prerequisites for obtaining a visa will all be covered in this part.

2.1 Transportation Options

Tallinn has excellent connections to both domestic and foreign locations, and it offers a range of transportation choices to match your tastes and price range. Here are the main methods for traveling to Tallinn:

2.1.1 By Air:

Tallinn Airport (TLL) is the primary entry point into the city for travelers arriving from overseas. It is a convenient way to travel to Tallinn because it is only 4 kilometers from the city center. With frequent flights to significant European cities, the airport serves a number of foreign carriers. To meet the needs of passengers, it provides cutting-edge amenities and services. Taxis, airport shuttle buses, and tram services are all readily available for getting from the airport to the city center.

2.1.2 By Sea:

Ferry Services: Tallinn is well connected to its surrounding nations by sea thanks to its advantageous location on the Baltic Sea. Between Tallinn and Stockholm, Sweden, as well as Helsinki, Finland, there are frequent ferry connections. Not only is the trip across the Baltic Sea convenient, but it also offers beautiful views of the coastline.

2.1.3 Land-based:

Bus and Train: Tallinn is easily reachable by bus or train from close-by nations including Latvia, Lithuania, and Russia. It is handy for visitors arriving by land because the city's main bus and train stations are situated near to the city center.

2.2 Airports and Terminals

The main entrance to the city is through Tallinn Airport, also known as Lennart Meri Tallinn Airport. It bears Lennart Meri's name, a well-known diplomat and former president of Estonia. Here are some crucial details regarding Tallinn Airport:

Services: A variety of services are available at Tallinn Airport to make your arrival and departure comfortable. You may discover restaurants, cafés, duty-free shops, vehicle rental agencies, and exchange bureaus.

Transportation to the City Center: It is easy to go from the airport to the city center. The tram, airport shuttle buses, and taxi services are all options. An inexpensive and effective option, the tram line offers a quick journey from the airport to the city center.

Customs and immigration: You must go through these processes when you arrive. In general, the procedure is quick and easy, especially if you have the required travel documents.

2.3 Visa and Entry Requirements

The fact that Estonia is a member of the European Union (EU) and the Schengen Area makes traveling easier for many tourists. It's imperative to understand the entry and visa procedures unique to your country of citizenship, though. An outline of Tallinn's visa and admission requirements is provided below:

You can enter Estonia for brief stays without a visa if you are a citizen of a Schengen Area nation. This makes travel inside the Schengen Area—which comprises the majority of the EU member states—smooth and easy.

Visa-Free Travel: For brief stays, typically up to 90 days over the course of 180 days, some nationalities outside of the Schengen Area are exempt from visa requirements. For the most recent information on visa requirements, visit the official website of the Estonian government or local neighborhood Estonian embassy or consulate.

Longer Stays: You may need to apply for a residence permit if you want to stay in Tallinn for an extended period of time, such as for employment or school. Consult the Estonian Police and Border Guard Board or the Estonian Ministry of Foreign Affairs for complete details on the conditions and procedures for getting a residency permit since they can differ.

Validity of Passport: Ensure that your passport is valid for at least three months after the day that you intend to depart from Estonia. Having a few blank pages for entry and exit stamps is also a good idea.

Border crossings: Travelers should be aware of any special entry requirements when crossing Estonia's land borders with Russia and Latvia.

Remember that visa and entry requirements are subject to change, so it's imperative to confirm the most recent details well in advance of your trip to Tallinn with the Estonian government or your country's embassy or consulate. Following the admission guidelines will make traveling to this intriguing Baltic city easy and hassle-free.

EXPLORING TALLINN

Tallinn has a wide range of sights and activities for visitors because of its extensive history and rich cultural heritage. An extensive guide to discovering the best of Tallinn is provided here, including everything from the Old Town's cobblestone alleyways to the tranquil beauty of Kadriorg Palace and Park:

3.1 Old Town

The Old Town, also known as "Vanalinn," in the center of Tallinn, is like a real-life fairy tale. This amazingly well-preserved medieval city center is home to a wealth of historical and architectural marvels and is a UNESCO World Heritage site.

Historical Allure: Entering the Old Town immediately transports you back in time. The city's long history is reflected in its Gothic and Renaissance-style architecture. Explore its maze-like cobblestone streets to find secret courtyards, historical structures, and breathtaking church spires.

Town Hall Square, also known as "Raekoja plats," is located in the center of Old Town and is a bustling gathering place because of its vibrant buildings, outdoor cafes, and the imposing Town Hall, which was built in the 13th century. This square serves as the main point for celebrations and activities, and the Tallinn Christmas Market brings the area to life during the holidays.

Cathedral Hill, where Toompea Castle and Alexander Nevsky Cathedral are located, dominates the skyline of Old Town. The Estonian Parliament is located in Toompea Castle, which also provides sweeping views of the city. With its characteristic onion domes, the stunning Russian Orthodox Alexander Nevsky Cathedral is a masterpiece of architecture.

Museums and Galleries: Tallinn's history and culture are revealed in the Old Town's numerous museums and galleries. The Tallinn City Museum, the Estonian History Museum, and the Kiek in de Kök Museum, which provides an underground view of the city's defenses, are all must-see locations.

Dining and shopping: Foodies and shoppers alike will find paradise in the Old Town. You may find delightful eateries, cafes, and pubs that serve both traditional Estonian food and other cuisines. With a wide selection of wool products, amber jewelry, and local crafts, the area is also ideal for souvenir shopping.

3.2 Kadriorg Palace and Park

A short distance from the Old Town, the Kadriorg Palace and Park offer a startling contrast to Tallinn's historic allure. Visitors can find peace and tranquility at this Baroque palace and in the park that surrounds it.

History and architecture: Peter the Great ordered the construction of Kadriorg Palace in the early

18th century. It is a beautiful example of Baroque architecture with its pink and white façade, elaborate stucco ornamentation, and rich interiors.

Parkland Beauty: The palace is located in the expansive Kadriorg Park, which has been expertly maintained with gardens, fountains, and strolling paths. Particularly in the spring and summer when the park is in full bloom, it's a great area for a leisurely stroll or a picnic.

KUMU Art Museum: One of Estonia's most recognized cultural institutions, the Kumu Art Museum is situated in the park. It holds a remarkable collection of Estonian art, both traditional and modern. The museum's eye-catching modern design is a draw in and of itself.

3.3 Toompea Hill

The Old Town's Toompea Hill is a location with political and historical significance. It is a location where the present and past collide and it provides stunning views of Tallinn.

Toompea Castle is positioned atop the hill and is also referred to as Tall Hermann Tower. It has served as a bastion for many years and now houses the Estonian Parliament. Viewing platforms offer visitors sweeping views of Tallinn and the Baltic Sea.

Pikk Hermann: The Estonian flag is flown from the Pikk Hermann Tower, which is next to Toompea Castle. This makes for an interesting sight, particularly during holidays. Every day at sunrise and dusk, the flag is raised and lowered according to a special custom.

Kohtuotsa Viewing Platform: On Toompea Hill, you can see one of Tallinn's most famous views from the Kohtuotsa Viewing Platform. The view includes the spires and crimson rooftops of the Old Town as well as the new metropolis beyond.

3.4 Museums and Galleries

Every traveler's interests can be met in Tallinn's diverse collection of museums and galleries, which has a thriving cultural environment.

The Kumu Art Museum is a highlight, as was already said, not simply for its artwork but also for its cutting-edge design. From the 18th century to the present, it presents a thorough collection of Estonian art.

The Seaplane Harbour houses the Estonian Maritime Museum, which chronicles Estonia's maritime history. It is renowned for housing a sizable collection of old ships and submarines. Some of these vessels can even be explored by visitors.

The Estonian Open Air Museum is an outdoor museum that displays the rural architecture and way of life in Estonia during many historical eras. It is situated in a beautiful seaside location. An immersive experience can be had by strolling among the genuine farmsteads, windmills, and village structures.

Tallinn City Museum: This museum provides a fascinating look into the past, present, and future of Tallinn. It's a fantastic location to discover how the city changed from its medieval origins to the present.

3.5 Parks and Green Spaces

Tallinn, while being an urban area, is peppered with parks and green areas that offer a welcome respite from the bustle of the city.

Kadriorg Park: As was already noted, Kadriorg Park is a wonderful illustration of a beautifully maintained green area. It is the ideal location for outdoor recreation and relaxation thanks to its fountains, ponds, and walking pathways.

Pirita Promenade: The Pirita neighborhood features a stunning seaside promenade along the Baltic Sea coastlines. It's a great place for a

Traditional Estonian flatbread known as karask is made from barley or rye flour. Usually served with butter and cheese and fried on a heated griddle.

Fish from Lake Peipsi, one of the biggest transboundary lakes in Europe, is famous for being of the highest caliber. Try the pike, perch, and vendace that are caught nearby. They frequently come with a side of potatoes and are fried.

4.2 Local Restaurants and Cafes

Tallinn has a thriving and varied restaurant scene with a variety of places to suit all tastes and price ranges. There are many options available, whether you prefer traditional Estonian food or cuisine from other countries.

Olde Hansa: If you want to have a genuine medieval eating experience, you must go there. The restaurant's vintage setting, which includes candles and costumed servers, adds to the Old

Town's allure. Try some of their filling wild game dishes, such as elk or wild boar.

Rataskaevu 16: Estonian food is served at this little eatery in the center of the Old Town. It's a terrific place to experience regional flavors and the menu frequently includes traditional meals with a contemporary touch.

Farm: If you enjoy farm-to-table cuisine, check out this restaurant in Tallinn that employs local, seasonal ingredients to make traditional Estonian dishes.

Von Krahli Aed: Located in a lovely courtyard, this restaurant offers a modern twist on Estonian food by fusing regional ingredients with global culinary fads.

Must Puudel is a trendy café in the center of Tallinn that is perfect if you're in the mood for something more relaxed. A simple dinner, cake, or coffee are all delicious here. The ambiance is laid-back, and the decor has a nostalgic feel.

Visit Kohvik Moon for a little of nostalgia and an experience that will look good on Instagram. This Soviet-era-inspired retro cafe serves delectable coffee and pastries while providing a window into the city's past.

4.3 Must-Try Dishes

Here are some must-try foods to relish as you explore Tallinn's culinary scene:

Sült: A typical Estonian appetizer, sult is a cold jelly dish prepared from pork or beef. It frequently comes with mustard and pickles.

Known as "hapukapsasupp," this sauerkraut soup is a favorite comfort meal in Estonia. Usually prepared with pork, it is served warm with sour cream.

Pirukad: Pirukad are savory pastries stuffed with a variety of ingredients, frequently rice, onions, and minced meat. They are delicious as a snack or light dinner.

The delicacy known as "beer and onion sausages," or "lle ja Sibulaseen," which mixes the richness of sausage with caramelized onions, is popular in the taverns of Tallinn.

Kohuke is a tasty treat that can be eaten for breakfast or as a snack. It's a chocolate-covered confection with quark within that comes in a variety of tastes.

Kohv: Don't forget to drink some Estonian coffee with your dinner. Excellent coffee options can be found all across Tallinn, where café culture is growing.

Try Vana Tallinn, a sweet and aromatic liqueur that is frequently consumed as an aperitif or used in cocktails, for a taste of the local booze.

Tallinn's diverse culinary scene offers visitors the chance to engage with Estonia's rich cultural heritage in addition to sampling exquisite cuisine. Tallinn is a distinctive and memorable culinary destination, and the city's eateries and cafes offer a delightful trip into the flavors and traditions that contribute to this.

ACCOMMODATION

A crucial step in trip preparation is picking the ideal lodging in Tallinn. The city provides a wide range of accommodations, including opulent hotels, affordable hostels, and distinctive vacation rentals. Here is a detailed look at the various lodging options available in Tallinn:

5.1 Hotels and Resorts

Tallinn has a wide range of hotels and resorts to suit all tastes and price ranges. There are options available to suit your needs, whether you're looking for cozy comfort or upscale luxury:

The Three Sisters Hotel is a boutique hotel located in the center of the Old Town and is housed in three painstakingly restored 14th-century merchant houses. It is renowned for its historical allure, opulent accommodations, and attentive service.

Swissôtel Tallinn is a modern luxury hotel with breath-taking views of the Tallinn skyline and the Baltic Sea. It is centrally located in the city. The hotel offers a spa, a variety of dining options, and chic rooms.

Nordic Hotel Forum: The Nordic Hotel Forum is a chic and contemporary hotel that is close to the Old Town district and the Rotermann Quarter. It has luxurious accommodations, an excellent spa, and a well-liked rooftop bar with sweeping views.

The Radisson Blu Sky Hotel is a high-rise establishment with cozy, roomy accommodations in the heart of Tallinn. On the hotel's 24th floor, the Sky Lounge offers breathtaking views of the city.

Pirita Spa Hotel: If you're seeking for a resort-style experience, the Pirita Spa Hotel, located by the sea, is a superb choice. It offers spa facilities, wellness treatments, and close access to Pirita Beach.

5.2 Hostels and Guesthouses

For budget-conscious tourists, hostels and guesthouses are wonderful options that nonetheless provide a comfortable and convivial environment:

Tallinn Backpackers Hostel: Located in the center of the Old Town, Tallinn Backpackers Hostel is recognized for its vibrant atmosphere and social activities. It's a terrific spot to meet fellow tourists and experience the city.

Red Emperor Hostel: Nestled within the Old Town, Red Emperor Hostel offers a pleasant and welcoming ambiance. The personnel are noted for their kindness and local knowledge.

OldHouse Hostel: OldHouse Hostel is a unique accommodation set in a medieval structure. It mixes the elegance of an old-world setting with modern facilities and a central position.

Mere Guesthouse: Located near the vibrant Telliskivi Creative City, Mere Guesthouse offers budget-friendly accommodation with clean and comfortable rooms. It's a convenient location for experiencing the city's artistic and cultural environment.

Economy Hotel: Situated close to Tallinn's bus terminal, Economy Hotel is a no-frills solution for those on a limited budget. The accommodations are simple but comfortable, and the location is accessible for visitors arriving by bus.

5.3 Airbnb and Vacation Rentals

Tallinn has seen a rise in the use of vacation rental sites like Airbnb, which give visitors the ability to live like a local while yet enjoying all the comforts of home away from home:

Several Airbnb hosts in Tallinn provide flats in the Old Town, including this delightful two-bedroom choice. You may tour the city's historical sites on foot if you stay in the center of it.

Cozy Wooden House: Staying in one of Tallinn's wooden houses would make for a more distinctive experience. These classic houses, many of which feature contemporary facilities, give a glimpse of the city's architectural past.

If you like contemporary luxury, you can find expensive vacation rentals with breathtaking sea views and tastefully decorated interiors. Modern Penthouse with Sea Views.

Bohemian Studio in Tallinn's Telliskivi Creative City, a hip neighborhood renowned for its creative energy. Being close to hip cafes, art galleries, and street art is a benefit of staying in a bohemian studio here.

Family-Friendly Vacation Home: Are you on a family vacation? Large homes and flats available as vacation rentals may accommodate large parties. The convenience of a kitchen and living area will be available to you.

The best place to stay in Tallinn will mostly rely on your interests, travel style, and budget. Tallinn offers a wide range of accommodations to make your stay pleasant and memorable, whether you like the luxury of a hotel, the friendliness of a hostel, or the intimacy of a vacation home. You will be surrounded by the city's rich history and vibrant culture wherever you decide to stay.

SHOPPING IN TALLINN

Tallinn is a wonderful location for those who love to shop in addition to being a city rich in history and culture. There are many options to explore, ranging from quaint markets and shops to busy retail areas.

6.1 Markets and Souvenirs

Finding unique presents to remember your vacation to Tallinn while exploring the local markets and looking for souvenirs is a great way to fully immerse yourself in the culture:

Tallinn Old Town Souvenir Market: This outdoor market, which is located in the center of the Old Town, is a veritable gold mine of trinkets and handmade goods. A wide variety of commodities, including woolen goods, ceramics, jewelry, and traditional Estonian handicrafts, are available here. The ideal place to purchase souvenirs to relive your time in Tallinn.

Balti Jaama Turg (Baltic Station Market) is a busy center of activity and is housed in a beautiful antique railroad market hall. It's a great place to enjoy regional cuisine and buy fresh meats, cheeses, and produce. Additionally, the market sells a range of artisanal goods and one-of-a-kind trinkets. Don't forget to check out Telliskivi Creative City, which is nearby and has trendy shops, cafes, and street art.

Nmme Market: This market offers a glimpse into daily life in the lovely neighborhood of Nmme, Estonia. It is renowned for its locally grown, fresh produce, which includes cheeses, fruits, and vegetables. Saturdays are when locals and tourists converge on the market to shop and take in the lively atmosphere.

The Rotermann Quarter's Estonian Design House is a store that features a variety of modern Estonian design. Here, you can find distinctive apparel, accessories, home decor, and more made by regional designers and artists. It's the perfect spot to locate unique items that showcase contemporary Estonian design.

6.2 Trendy Boutiques

Trendy stores in Tallinn provide a variety of domestic and foreign fashion, design, and lifestyle goods. Discovering the city's glamorous side through these chic stores:

The Old Town's Reede shop specializes in designer apparel, accessories, and home goods. The store is a chic destination for individuals looking for one-of-a-kind items thanks to its well curated collection of regional and international brands.

Tallinn Dolls is the place to go if you're looking for traditional Estonian handicrafts with a contemporary touch. Along with other regional products, the store sells an outstanding selection of handmade dolls dressed in traditional Estonian garb.

Rahva Raamat Bookstore features a designated area for design and lifestyle products in addition to its amazing collection of books. Browse a selection of chic presents, such as stationery, stationery from Scandinavia, and more.

Eesti Disain House is a Rotermann Quarter independent concept store that specializes in Estonian design. It provides a wide selection of items for the home, apparel, and accessories, all made by Estonian designers. The store offers a venue for upcoming regional artists to exhibit their work.

6.3 Shopping Streets

Tallinn has bustling shopping areas where you may meander, explore, and find a variety of stores, from national chains to independent stores:

Viru Street is one of the most well-known shopping avenues in Tallinn and is situated right in the middle of the city. A variety of multinational brands, department stores, and neighborhood retailers may be found here. It is a thriving center for dining, shopping, and entertainment.

Pikk Street: The Old Town's Pikk Street is renowned for its boutique stores. For collectors and art enthusiasts, it's the ideal location to visit nearby art galleries, vintage shops, and craft boutiques.

A hidden treasure in the Old Town, Müürivahe Street is home to a number of artisanal shops, including pottery workshops, art galleries, and jewelry stores. Shopping on Müürivahe Street is a quieter, more personal experience.

Rataskaevu Street: This street, which is close to the Town Hall Square, has a variety of independent shops, eateries, and quaint cafes. It's a fun spot to explore while looking for unusual products and eating.

The shopping scene in Tallinn offers a charming blend of heritage and innovation. The city's marketplaces, boutiques, and shopping districts are where you may discover authentic Estonian mementos, designer clothing, and unique finds. It's a fantastic opportunity to bring a little bit of Tallinn's vivacious culture and fashion home with you.

NIGHTLIFE AND ENTERTAINMENT

The nightlife in Tallinn is as vibrant and diverse as its culture and history. The city offers a variety of options to keep you occupied far into the night, from lovely bars and traditional pubs to vibrant nightclubs and compelling cultural shows.

7.1 Bars and Pubs

The bars and pubs in Tallinn offer the perfect atmosphere for spending a relaxed evening with friends or taking in the local scene. Consider these notable locations:

Hell Hunt: Opened in 1993, Hell Hunt is one of Tallinn's oldest bars. It is well known for its wide assortment of beers, inviting environment, and intimate setting. The bar also serves delectable pub fare, including traditional Estonian cuisine.

Prgu, which means "Hell," offers a setting in the style of the Middle Ages and a sizable assortment of craft brews. The bar is well-known for its robust fare, which includes meals made with wild boar and elk. This makes it the ideal place to combine traditional Estonian food with top-notch brews.

Drink Bar & Grill is a chic and contemporary spot for gourmet food and cocktails that is close to Town Hall Square. For those looking for a more posh and elegant setting, it's a terrific option.

Valli Baar is a storied dive bar that has grown to be a recognized landmark in Tallinn. For those who value a traditional bar environment, it delivers an authentic experience with its unpretentious interior and reasonably priced drinks.

Pirita Beach Bar: If you're traveling in the summer, Pirita Beach Bar is where you may sip cool cocktails while taking in views of the ocean. The bar is a great place to unwind throughout the summer because of its tranquil coastal setting.

7.2 Nightclubs

Tallinn provides a range of nightclubs with various themes and musical genres for those wishing to party the night away and experience the city's thriving club scene:

Club Hollywood: One of Tallinn's biggest and most well-known nightclubs, Club Hollywood is renowned for its upbeat vibe, great DJs, and broad range of music. It frequently holds energetic theme parties and performers from throughout the world.

Vabank: In the center of the Old Town, there is a hip nightclub called Vabank. It is a chic location for dancing and socializing because of its distinctive interior design, a blend of modern and medieval aesthetics.

Studio: Studio is a multipurpose club that regularly hosts a range of events, including cultural shows, DJ parties, and live concerts. The club's laid-back and welcoming ambiance draws in a wide range of customers.

Cuba Bar & Café: If you're in the mood for salsa dancing and Latin rhythms, this is the spot for you. Live music and dance performances are available at this establishment with a Cuban theme, and Cuban food and drinks are also available.

The well-known electronic music club Temple is situated in the Rotermann Quarter. It draws a large group of ardent music fans who come to experience the top DJs from around the world and the local scene.

7.3 Cultural Performances

Tallinn has a vibrant cultural scene, and there are many places to catch enthralling performances:

Estonian National Opera: The Estonian National Opera presents a wide range of opera, ballet, and classical music performances. It is housed in a spectacular structure in the center of the city. The venue's lavish décor and top-notch performances provide an unforgettable cultural experience.

Kanuti Gildi SAAL is a modern performing arts venue in Tallinn that specializes in interdisciplinary performances and experimental theater. It serves as a focal point for cutting-edge and stimulating cultural activities.

Nuku Theatre: For those drawn to puppetry and visual theater, Nuku Theatre is the ideal stop. The theater produces several performances for audiences of all ages that combine tradition and modernity.

Tallinn's Philarmonia is a concert venue that features symphony orchestra performances, chamber music events, and concerts of classical music. If you want to hear classical music in Tallinn, this is the place to go.

The Von Krahl Theatre is a well-known theater and performing arts center in Tallinn, known for its cutting-edge theater performances and avant-garde plays. It's a great option for people who want to learn more about modern theater and experimental shows.

Tallinn's nightlife and entertainment options appeal to a wide range of people, whether you want to unwind in a quiet bar, party the night away in a lively nightclub, or take in thought-provoking cultural acts. Your visit will be richer and more memorable thanks to the city's vibrant nightlife and cultural scene.

DAY TRIPS FROM TALLINN

The Estonian countryside is just as fascinating as Tallinn, which has a plethora of historical and cultural attractions. You may take day trips from Tallinn to see a variety of locations, including beautiful national parks, charming islands, and old coastal villages.

8.1 Lahemaa National Park

Lahemaa National Park is a stunning natural area that is only a short drive from Tallinn, making it the perfect day trip destination. This national park, which is the biggest in Estonia, offers a stunning and varied terrain with thick woods, gorgeous bogs, and alluring shoreline. What to anticipate when traveling to Lahemaa is as follows:

Visit the highest waterfall in Estonia, Jägala Waterfall, as your first stop on your adventure. When the water flow is at its highest in the spring, this natural wonder is exceptionally striking.

Lace up your hiking boots and take a stroll along the boardwalks of Viru Bog to learn more about the distinct and vulnerable ecosystem of a raised bog. Simply stunning views of the nearby marshes and forest may be found here.

Käsmu Maritime Museum: Due to its maritime heritage, Käsmu, a charming coastal village in Lahemaa, is frequently referred to as the "Captain's Village". Learn about the village's seafaring history and discover historical items by visiting the Käsmu Maritime Museum.

The Altja Fishing Village is a living museum that offers a glimpse of Estonia's traditional coastal way of life. It is a charming and educational stay because of the well-preserved structures and the lovely surroundings along the ocean.

Palmse Manor: Palmse Manor, a beautiful 18th-century mansion that provides insights into the lives of Estonia's nobility, is a perfect way to cap off your Lahemaa tour. The manor is a fascinating historical attraction because of its verdant lawn and wonderfully restored interiors.

8.2 Saaremaa Island

The largest island in Estonia, Saaremaa Island, is a great day trip from Tallinn. Saaremaa offers a tranquil retreat from the city and is well-known for its breathtaking natural beauty, historical attractions, and distinctive culture. Here are some things you can do on Saaremaa:

Kuressaare: Kuressaare, the capital of Saaremaa, is well-known for its preserved medieval fortress, Kuressaare Castle. Discover the town's quaint streets and the castle's grounds. The island's capital city also has a variety of restaurants and boutiques selling regional goods.

One of the most well-known meteorite craters in Europe is located in Saaremaa, the Kaali Meteorite Craters. There is a tourist center where you may learn more about the Kaali Meteorite Craters, a distinctive geological feature worth visiting.

Angla Windmill Hill is an outdoor museum that houses a number of conventional windmills. It's a beautiful location that sheds light on the island's agricultural history.

Panga Cliffs: For breath-taking views of the Baltic Sea, travel to Panga Cliffs on Saaremaa's northern coast. It's a great place to soak in the natural beauty of the island and wander leisurely along the cliffs.

For those who enjoy the outdoors, Vilsandi National Park on Saaremaa is a must-see location. This national park is renowned for its beautiful coastline vistas and varied birds. It is a sanctuary for trekking and birdwatching.

8.3 Paldiski and Pakri Peninsula

In addition to providing a look into Estonia's maritime and military past, Paldiski and the surrounding Pakri Peninsula offer stunning coastline beauty. On this day excursion, you can explore the following:

Paldiski seaside Cliffs: Paldiski is a picturesque seaside town with a rich history. The Paldiski Coastal Cliffs, which provide breathtaking views of the Baltic Sea and the surroundings, are a great place to start your day excursion.

Visit the Pakri Lighthouse, which is situated on the Pakri Peninsula. It is a well-known maritime landmark that offers a great vantage point from which to take in expansive views of the coastline.

Pakri Peninsula Nature Reserve: There are many different types of landscapes in the Pakri Peninsula Nature Reserve, including wetlands, woods, and coastal regions. It's a fantastic location for birds and trekking.

Submarine Base in Paldiski: Paldiski once served as the location of a Soviet submarine base. You can look around the ruins of this Cold War-era installation and learn about its history, but you cannot visit the base itself.

Padise Abbey: Padise Abbey is a well-preserved medieval monastery with a fascinating history that you might want to stop at on your way back to Tallinn. The abbey is situated in a lovely rural area.

You may discover the great diversity of Estonia's landscapes, history, and culture by visiting these day trip locations from Tallinn. Each day excursion provides a different adventure, whether you decide to meander through pristine national parks, study the historic architecture of islands, or learn about the nautical and military history of coastal cities.

CHRISTMAS IN TALLINN

During the Christmas season, Tallinn truly comes to life, transforming into a winter paradise with dazzling decorations, happy celebrations, and a magical ambiance. What to expect over Christmas in this wonderful city is as follows:

9.1 Christmas Markets

The Christmas Markets in Tallinn are a festive season highlight. These seasonal markets have the ideal setting in the Old Town, which features medieval architecture and cobblestone streets:

Tallinn Christmas Market: The Tallinn Christmas Market is the focal point of the city's holiday celebrations, and it is situated at Town Hall Square. Normally, the market begins in late November and runs through early January. There are rows of charming, wooden kiosks decorated with bright lights that sell an assortment of crafts, presents, and regional delicacies.

Explore the Estonian Christmas Market, which is located in the Rotermann Quarter, in addition to the main market. The greatest of Estonian craftsmanship, design, and food are on display at this market. It's a great place to find unusual presents and taste regional cuisine.

St. Catherine's Passage has a quaint market every year during the Christmas season. St. Catherine's Passage is a charming, congested lane in the Old Town. You can buy handmade items and traditional Estonian crafts here.

The Noblessner Christmas Market, which is situated in the hip Noblessner neighborhood, provides a more contemporary and urban Christmas experience. It has food stands, craft stands, and a variety of entertainment options.

9.2 Festive Traditions

Tallinn's Christmas customs have a strong Estonian cultural foundation. Some of the traditions and rituals you can come upon are listed below:

Advent Candles: In Tallinn, Advent is a significant aspect of the Christmas season. Each Sunday leading up to Christmas, many homes light an Advent candle, with the last candle being lit on Christmas Eve. This ceremony serves as a reminder of the coming of the Christ child.

Santa Claus, or Juluvana, makes house visits in Estonia on Christmas Eve to bring presents to the kids. Children eagerly await the arrival of Juluvana, who is often clothed in crimson and is accompanied by his servants, who are frequently referred to as "krampus" or "päkapikud."

Traditional Foods: On Christmas Eve, Estonians have a joyful holiday supper that includes roast pork, potatoes, sauerkraut, and blood sausage. Other well-liked Christmas foods include cranberry sauce and gingerbread cookies.

Christmas sauna: As part of their holiday custom, many Estonians unwind in a soothing sauna on Christmas Eve. It is regarded as a technique to purify the body and soul in preparation for the new year.

9.3 Holiday Events and Activities

Tallinn offers a variety of holiday activities and events that spread seasonal pleasure in addition to its Christmas markets and customs:

Christmas Concerts: Choirs, orchestras, and soloists frequently perform at Christmas concerts held in the city's churches and music halls. These performances produce a peaceful and cheerful ambience that perfectly encapsulates the spirit of the time of year.

Ice skating: The Old Town ice rink is a well-liked Christmastime destination. Visitors of all ages will love this location for some outdoor ice skating and the festive ambiance.

Candlelit Tours: During the holiday season, some historical sites and museums provide candlelit tours. You can learn more about Tallinn's history with this special experience.

Holiday Lights & Decorations: The streets and buildings of Tallinn are exquisitely decked out in glistening lights and festive accents. A must-do during the holiday season is to stroll through the lit Old Town.

Christmas Tree Lighting Ceremony: The Town Hall Square's yearly Christmas tree lighting ceremony ushers in the holiday season in a spectacular way. The square is buzzing with music, entertainment, and happy festivities as the tree is exquisitely decked.

Family-friendly Activities: There are a number of events and workshops available for families traveling with kids to keep the little ones occupied and in the holiday spirit. Examples include gingerbread decorating and craft making.

Tallinn's Christmas celebrations are a mash-up of age-old traditions, charming marketplaces, and joyous occasions that encapsulate the spirit of the season. The city's holiday spirit is certain to warm your heart and make memorable memories, whether you're looking for one-of-a-kind gifts at the markets, savoring a hearty meal in a neighborhood restaurant, or attending a Christmas symphony.

PRACTICAL INFORMATION

To ensure a seamless and pleasurable vacation, it's imperative to have a solid understanding of practical knowledge before visiting Tallinn. Here are some important factors to think about:

10.1 Language and Communication

Language: Tallinn has a large Estonian-speaking population and speaks Estonian as its official language. In tourist areas, hotels, and eateries in particular, English is also widely spoken and understood. There are a few other languages you might encounter, including German, Finnish, and Russian.

Communication: Estonia's infrastructure for communication is up to date and well-developed. What you need to know is this:

Mobile Networks: The mobile network coverage in Estonia is very good. Prepaid data plans are reasonably priced, and local SIM cards are easily accessible. If your carrier allows it, you can use your own phone with a local SIM or choose international roaming.

Free Wi-Fi is generally offered at Tallinn's hotels, cafes, restaurants, and public areas. During your visit, staying connected won't be a problem.

Dial 112 to contact the police, the fire department, or medical personnel in an emergency.

10.2 Currency and Money Matters

The Euro (EUR) is the official currency of Estonia. ATMs are generally available, and credit and debit cards are commonly accepted. Here are some crucial financial factors to remember:

Exchange of Money: You can exchange money at ATMs, banks, and currency exchange companies. While it is handy to withdraw money in Euros from an ATM, be aware of potential bank costs.

Credit Cards: The majority of establishments, including shops, eateries, and hotels, accept major credit and debit cards, such as Visa and Mastercard. For modest transactions and in case you visit locations where cards are not accepted, it is good to have some cash on hand.

Tipping: Tipping is expected but not required in Tallinn. Restaurant invoices frequently include service fees. It is customary to leave a gratuity of 10% to 15% of the total cost if service is not included. Rounding up the tab or leaving tiny change is appreciated in pubs and cafes.

10.3 Safety and Emergency Contacts

Tallinn is typically regarded as a secure location for tourists. However, it's always important to pay attention to your surroundings and use caution. What you need to know about safety and emergency contacts is as follows:

Emergency Services: In the event of an emergency, dial 112 to contact the police, the fire department, or the ambulance service. Any phone, including mobile phones, can be used to call this toll-free number.

Crime: Tallinn has a low rate of violent crime, and visitors are thought to feel safe there. However, petty theft can happen anywhere, especially in busy places or on public transportation. Keep an eye on your possessions and refrain from flaunting pricey stuff in public.

Travel Insurance: It is advised to have all-inclusive travel insurance that protects against theft, medical costs, and other unforeseen circumstances. Make sure your insurance is active throughout your entire vacation.

Health and Safety: The clean and secure atmosphere in Tallinn is well-known. Drinking tap water is safe, and hygiene requirements are strict. Additionally, it's a good idea to have all required vaccines current before traveling.

Modern hospitals and medical facilities are available in Tallinn, and the city's medical staff is well-trained. Holders of an EHIC are entitled to necessary medical care under the EU's reciprocal healthcare agreements.

Transportation Security: The public transportation system in Tallinn is generally reliable and effective. On trams and buses, be careful with your possessions, especially during rush hour. It is advised to use registered taxis as they are trustworthy and safe.

Consular Contacts: If you require consular service, you can get it through your nation's embassy or consulate in Tallinn.

Tallinn is a popular tourism destination because of its warm and welcoming attitude. You may make the most of your trip and guarantee a great and secure stay in this lovely Baltic city by being aware of these practical considerations.

ITINERARIES

It's important to arrange your itinerary for your time in Tallinn based on how long you'll be there. To help you make the most of your time in the city, the following suggested itineraries are provided:

11.1 One Day in Tallinn

If you only have one day to tour Tallinn, you may see the main attractions and experience the city's charm, culture, and history. Here is a suggested schedule for one day:

Start your day in the center of Tallinn's Old Town, a UNESCO World Heritage site, from 9:00 am to 12:00 pm. Observe the magnificent architecture of the Alexander Nevsky Cathedral, a famous Russian Orthodox cathedral. Take a leisurely stroll through the cobblestone streets, see the historic buildings, and enjoy the expansive views from Toompea Hill.

Lunch (12:00 PM – 1:00 PM): Enjoy a traditional Estonian meal at one of the Old Town's attractive cafes or eateries. Try some meals like elk stew, black bread, and herring.

Afternoon (1:00 PM - 4:00 PM): Continue your exploration by going to Town Hall Square, where you can find the Town Hall and one of Europe's oldest pharmacies, the Town Hall Pharmacy. Explore the square and its bustling neighborhood.

Late afternoon (4:00–6:00 PM): Take a leisurely stroll around the Old Town's lovely streets, where you may find a wide variety of boutiques, gift shops, and art galleries. Explore St. Catherine's Passage, which is renowned for its artisan studios.

supper (6:00–8:00 PM): For supper, enjoy Estonian cuisine in one of the quaint eateries in the Old Town. Try foods like kama, a typical dessert, and verivorst, a blood sausage.

Evening (8:00 PM and Upward): As dusk falls, stop by a neighborhood pub or cafe to take in the city's nightlife. You can select from a variety of venues in the Tallinn Old Town's thriving nightlife scene depending on your tastes.

11.2 Weekend Getaway

You can learn more about Tallinn's history, culture, and surroundings by spending a weekend there. An agenda for a special weekend getaway is provided below:

Day 1:

Morning (9 a.m. to 12 p.m.): Begin your weekend by visiting the Old Town's historical landmarks. Go to Toompea Castle, where the Estonian Parliament is located. From the Kohtuotsa Viewing Platform, take in the expansive views.

Dine at a restaurant with a view of the Old Town for lunch (12:30–1:30 PM). Enjoy traditional

Estonian fare like herring and mulgipuder (potato porridge).

The Kadriorg Palace and Park can be visited in the afternoon (from 1:00 to 4:00). Visit the Kadriorg Art Museum, stroll through the well-kept gardens, and explore the lovely Baroque palace.

Day 2:

Morning (9 AM–12 PM): Visit the Seaplane Harbour, a renowned maritime museum, in the morning. Explore seaplanes, learn about Estonia's maritime heritage, and get hands-on with the displays.

Lunch is served from 12:00 PM to 1:00 PM in the restaurant at Seaplane Harbour.

Afternoon (1:00 PM - 4:00 PM): Enjoy a leisurely stroll around the cosmopolitan area known as Telliskivi Creative City. Visit galleries, see the street art, and peruse the specialized stores.

Return to the Old Town in the late afternoon (4:00–6:00) and check out the KGB Museum in the Hotel Viru. Discover the Soviet era history of Tallinn and the secret KGB spying technology.

supper (6:00 PM–8:00 PM): Enjoy a delicious supper at a restaurant of your choice to round off your weekend while sampling the many culinary wonders of Tallinn.

11.3 Family-Friendly Adventures

Tallinn is a great vacation spot for families because it has a variety of things to do and attractions for people of all ages. Here is a schedule for a fun family adventure:

Day 1:

Early in the morning (9 a.m. to 12 p.m.): Start your family vacation with a trip to the Tallinn

Zoo. Investigate the numerous animal displays and take in a picnic in the lovely park.

Lunch (12:30–1:30): Bring a picnic lunch to the zoo or choose a local eatery that welcomes children.

Visit the Estonian Open Air Museum in the afternoon (from 1:00 PM to 4:00 PM). Through interactive exhibits, the museum offers a close-up look at rural culture and living in Estonia.

Day 2:

Morning (9 a.m. to noon): Board a ferry towards the lovely island of Prangli. Discover the island's natural splendor, stroll along the sandy beaches, and spend some quality time outside with your family.

Lunch (12:00–1:00 PM): Take a picnic on Prangli Island or eat at a nearby restaurant.

Return to the mainland in the afternoon (12:30–4:00) and stop by the NUKU Puppet Theatre and Museum. With puppet shows and engaging exhibitions, it's a fun experience for both children and adults.

The youngsters can play in the playgrounds and open areas of Kadriorg Park in the late afternoon (4:00–6:00 PM). Swan Pond, a picturesque location, is another option.

Dinner is served from 6:00 PM to 8:00 PM at a kid-friendly restaurant in Tallinn's Kadriorg neighborhood.

These suggested itineraries can be modified to fit your interests and preferences because they are adaptable. The city of Tallinn offers a wide variety of experiences that may accommodate different travel styles and lengths of time, whether you're visiting for a day, a weekend, or a family vacation.

CONCLUSION

Without a doubt, your trip to Tallinn, Estonia, was a remarkable one that was rich in history, culture, and beautiful scenery. Let's review the main points of this guide as we draw to a close and speculate about your potential return to Tallinn in the future:

12.1 Recap and Highlights

Tallinn has a lot to offer, including its Old Town, which has been restored, as well as its thriving cultural scene, lovely parks, and intriguing history. Here is a list of some of the highlights and activities you might have had while here:

Old Town Charm: The Old Town, located in the city's center, offers a mesmerizing backdrop for your travels with its medieval architecture, cobblestone streets, and charming squares.

You may have visited ancient sites like Toompea Castle, Alexander Nevsky Cathedral, and the

Town Hall, which all helped to shape Tallinn's distinctive personality.

Cultural Treasures: You can fully immerse yourself in Estonian culture and art in Tallinn, which is home to a wide variety of museums, galleries, and theaters.

Natural Beauty: Tallinn's parks and natural spaces, such as Kadriorg Park and the Seaplane Harbour, offer a welcome retreat into nature, and the city's coastal regions offer breathtaking vistas and leisure activities.

Christmas Magic: If you had come during the holiday season, you would have enjoyed Tallinn's lovely Christmas markets, joyous customs, and lively atmosphere.

Culinary Highlights: Your trip has probably been made even more enjoyable by Estonian cuisine, with its hearty dishes and distinctive flavors. The customary blood sausage, herring, and delectable gingerbread cookies should not be overlooked.

Adventures for Families: The Tallinn Zoo, the Estonian Open Air Museum, and the NUKU Puppet Theatre all provide family-friendly activities that are both entertaining and instructive.

Modern Culture: You may get a glimpse of Tallinn's developing cultural landscape by visiting the hip Telliskivi Creative City and the artistic Noblessner neighborhood.

12.2 Looking Forward to Your Return

As your trip to Tallinn comes to an end, you might feel compelled to visit this alluring city once more in the future. Here are some things to think about as you prepare for your upcoming trip:

Unfinished Adventures: With so much to discover, a single trip to Tallinn might not be sufficient. There may be adventures on your next visit that you won't have time for this time.

Seasonal Changes: Going back at a different time of year can give you a new perspective. Tallinn undergoes seasonal transformations and presents fresh opportunities.

Deeper Exploration: Get to know the locals, immerse yourself in Tallinn's culture, and explore the city's history.

Festivals & Events: Throughout the year, Tallinn holds a number of festivals and events. To time your homecoming with something spectacular, research forthcoming events.

Consider extending your trip to neighboring Baltic capitals like Riga and Vilnius, or take a ferry to see adjacent islands, for example.

Reconnect with Favorites: Visit your favorite places and eateries once again and enjoy the coziness and comfort of a place you've grown to love.

Whether you're looking for history, culture, untouched natural beauty, or just a peaceful getaway, Tallinn is a city that has something to offer every traveler. The next stage in your investigation of Tallinn's charms will certainly be your return to this endearing Baltic jewel. To whet your appetite for the adventures that are yet to come in this timeless city, let your recollections of Tallinn's ancient streets, festive marketplaces, and friendly friendliness.

Bonus: Useful phrases

Here are 50 useful phrases you might hear or use while in Tallinn in 2023:

- Tere hommikust! - Good morning!
- Tere päevast! - Good day!
- Tere õhtust! - Good evening!
- Head ööd! - Good night!
- Tere tulemast Tallinna! - Welcome to Tallinn!
- Kuidas ma saan sind aidata? - How can I help you?
- Palun - Please
- Aitäh - Thank you
- Palun vabandust - Excuse me
- Jah - Yes
- Ei - No
- Mitu maksab see? - How much does this cost?
- Kas sul on inglisekeelne menüü? - Do you have an English menu?
- Ma ei räägi eesti keelt - I don't speak Estonian

- Ma räägin inglise keelt - I speak English
- Kuidas ma saan Vanalinnani? - How do I get to the Old Town?
- Kus asub bussi- / trammipeatus? - Where is the bus/tram stop?
- Kas saaksite mind hotelli juhatada? - Can you direct me to the hotel?
- Ma olen kaotanud oma passi - I've lost my passport
- Mul on vaja arsti - I need a doctor
- Kas sa oskad mind aidata? - Can you help me?
- Kust ma leian lähima apteegi? - Where can I find the nearest pharmacy?
- Ma tahaksin tellida ühe kohvi - I'd like to order one coffee
- Kas teil on gluteenivaba menüü? - Do you have a gluten-free menu?
- Võib ma paluda arvet? - May I have the check, please?
- Millal see avatakse/suletakse? - When does this open/close?
- Kus asub lähim pank? - Where is the nearest bank?

- Mul on broneering number [number] - I have a reservation number [number]
- Kui palju maksab takso lennujaama? - How much is the taxi to the airport?
- Mis kell on nüüd? - What time is it now?
- Kas sa oskad mind rääkida? - Can you tell me the way?
- Kas saaksite mulle anda ühe tualetti? - Can you show me to the restroom?
- Kas sul on mobiiltelefoni laadija? - Do you have a mobile phone charger?
- Ma ei tea - I don't know
- Sa oled väga sõbralik - You're very friendly
- See on väga maitsev - This is very delicious
- Kuidas su nimi on? - What's your name?
- Mulle meeldib see koht - I like this place
- Ma armastan Tallinna - I love Tallinn
- Kas sulle meeldib siin elada? - Do you like living here?
- See on kaunis linn - This is a beautiful city

- Kas sul on soovitusi, mida teha? - Do you have any recommendations for things to do?
- Ma armastan seda vaadet - I love this view
- Mis on ilmaennustus? - What's the weather forecast?
- Kus asub lähim turistiteave? - Where is the nearest tourist information?
- Ma otsin Kingituste poodi - I'm looking for a gift shop
- Kas saate mind pildistada? - Can you take a photo of me?
- Ma tahan maitsta Eesti toitu - I want to try Estonian food
- Kui palju maksab sissepääs? - How much is the entrance fee?
- Head reisi! - Have a good trip!

Printed in Great Britain
by Amazon

32243235R00050